HISTORY OF
JAZZ

THIS EDITION

Editorial Management by Oriel Square
Produced for DK by WonderLab Group LLC
Jennifer Emmett, Erica Green, Kate Hale, *Founders*

Editor Maya Myers; **Photography Editor** Nicole DiMella; **Managing Editor** Rachel Houghton;
Designers Project Design Company; **Researcher** Michelle Harris; **Copy Editor** Lori Merritt; **Indexer** Connie Binder;
Proofreader Susan K. Hom; **Sensitivity Reader** Ebonye Gussine Wilkins;
Series Reading Specialist Dr. Jennifer Albro; **Jazz Historian and Consultant** Mark Stryker

First American Edition, 2024
Published in the United States by DK Publishing, a division of Penguin Random House LLC
1745 Broadway, 20th Floor, New York, NY 10019

A catalog record for this book is available from the Library of Congress.
HC ISBN: 978-0-7440-9455-8
PB ISBN: 978-0-7440-9454-1

DK books are available at special discounts when purchased in bulk for sales promotions, premiums, fund-raising, or educational use.
For details, contact:
DK Publishing Special Markets, 1745 Broadway, 20th Floor, New York, NY 10019
SpecialSales@dk.com

Printed and bound in China

The publisher would like to thank the following for their kind permission to reproduce their images:
a=above; c=center; b=below; l=left; r=right; t=top; b/g=background

123RF.com: alekseiderin 18-19b, 26-27b, 30-31b, 34-35b, 38-39b, 42-43b, 46-47b, 52-53b, 56-57b, 60-61b; **Alamy Stock Photo:** 16tl, Album 11crb,
14cr, 32cl, 37tr, Allstar Picture Library Limited 47tr, Auk Archive 55tr, Ira Berger 39c, Imma Casanellas 59clb, Classicstock / H. Armstrong Roberts
22-23 (Background), dcphoto 44tl, Everett Collection Historical 33tr, Everett Collection Inc 28-29, 51tr, Glasshouse Images / Circa Images 20tl,
GRANGER – Historical Picture Archive 15tl, 24-25 (Background), Phillip Harrington 48cla, Hemis / Renault Philippe 57tr, Heritage Image Partnership
Ltd / National Jazz Archive 52cb, IanDagnall Computing 17c, Lebrecht Music & Arts 20-21b, Lifestyle pictures 61tr, North Wind Picture Archives
12clb, PA Images 31tl, Photo 12 / Archives du 7e Art collection 14b, Photo-Fox 50c, Photo12 / Coll-DITE / USIS 30cla, Pictorial Press Ltd 16-17t, 17tr,
23c, 25tc, 29tr, 54bc, ZUMA Press, Inc. 60-61t; **Collection of the Smithsonian National Museum of African American History and Culture:** 8bl;
Depositphotos Inc: Estudiosaavedra 39tr, Prikhnenko 14-15; **Dreamstime.com:** Martin Cambriglia 4-5, Dtvector 36 (Background), 38-39
(Background), Evgenii89 6-7, Firststar 9tr, Jiawangkun 18-19, Lebedinski 16b, Nadiaaudigiephotography 46-47 (Background), Christian Ouellet 10cl,
Anastasija Panfilova 58-59 (Background), Felix Pergande 42-43 (Background), Photographerlondon 8-9, Anzhelika Poltavets 50-51 (Background),
I Nyoman Trianto Putrayana 48-49 (Background), Sharpshot 26-27 (Background), Shutterfree, Llc / R. Gino Santa Maria 34tl, Anton Starikov 36bc,
Venusangel 36cl, Mitar Vidakovic 10-11; **Getty Images:** Archive Photos / Gene Lester 34c, Archive Photos / Hulton Archive 24tl, 24tr, Archive Photos
/ Hulton Archive / Stringer 30crb, Archive Photos / Jack Vartoogian 41t, 49tl, Archive Photos / PhotoQuest 11cla, Archive Photos / Stringer 53tr,
Bettmann 24br, CBS Photo Archive 32tl, Stephen J. Cohen 58tl, Corbis Historical 19, Gamma-Keystone / Keystone-France 41bl, Erika Goldring 12-13,
49bl, Frazer Harrison 35tr, Hulton Archive / Archivio Cameraphoto Epoche 46tr, Hulton Archive / Bob Parent 6, Hulton Archive / Keystone / Stringer
31ca, INA 49tr, Keystone-France / Gamma-Rapho 11cb, Douglas Mason 1, 59t, Michael Ochs Archives 15cra, Michael Ochs Archives / Donaldson
Collection 43tr, 45tc, 46c, 51c, 51cb, Michael Ochs Archives / Icon and Image 42tr, Michael Ochs Archives / Stringer 25tr, 27t, 27cr, 33bc, 35ca, 45bc,
47tc, 48br, 51crb, 52cr, 55tl, Michael Ochs Archives / Tom Copi 55c, Moviepix / John Kobal Foundation 23tc, New York Daily News Archive 43crb,
Robertus Pudyanto 56cla, 56-57, Redfern / David Redfern 50tl, Redferns / Andrew Lepley 47cla, Redferns / C Brandon 11cr, Redferns / David
Redfern 41b, 50tc, 53cb, Redferns / Gai Terrell 40tl, Redferns / Gilles Petard 22cra, 26cl, 39cb, 45tr, Redferns / JP Jazz Archive 18crb, 23tr, 53ca,
Redferns / Paul Hoeffler 46crb, Universal Images Group / VW Pics 58b, WireImage / Tim Mosenfelder 13tr; **Getty Images / iStock:** Vitalii
Abakumov 60tl, E+ / FG Trade 61cb, E+ / Recep-Bg 34-35 (Background), Fstop123 21cra, st_lux 10clb, tereks 7; **Image Courtesy of International
Military Antiques, Inc. IMA-USA.com:** 33br; **Library of Congress, Washington, D.C.:** Gottlieb, William P. — 1917 3, 11c, William P. Gottlieb 22br,
26c, 32bl, 37, William P. Gottlieb 38tl, 40br, 42tl, 54crb, William P. Gottlieb / Ira and Leonore S. Gershwin Fund Collection, Music Division, 38c;
Courtesy of National Park Service, USA: Hunter Miles Davis 12tl; **National Museum of American History / Smithsonian Institution:** 28tl;
The New York Public Library: Music Division, The New York Public Library. "Maple leaf rag" The New York Public Library Digital Collections. 1899.
https://digitalcollections.nypl.org/items/510d47da-538d-a3d9-e040-e00a18064a99 14tl, Music Division, The New York Public Library. "Tiger rag :
one step" The New York Public Library Digital Collections. 1917. https://digitalcollections.nypl.org/items/510d47da-4f93-a3d9-e040-
e00a18064a99 30-31; **Photograph by Art Kane - Courtesy © Art Kane Archive:** 44b; **Sheridan Libraries, Johns Hopkins University:** Leo Feist,
Inc. / E. Pfeiffer, N.Y. 10c, Whitney-Warner Pub. Co. / By Chauncey Haines 10cb; **Shutterstock.com:** Andrei Minsk 54-55 (Background);
The US National Archives and Records Administration: 54tl

Cover images: *Front:* **Dreamstime.com:** Martin Cambriglia (Backgroud); **Getty Images:** Redferns / JP Jazz Archive b;
Back: **Dreamstime.com:** Yifang Zhao clb

All other images © Dorling Kindersley Limited
For more information see: www.dkimages.com

www.dk.com

Level
4

HISTORY OF
JAZZ

Melissa H. Mwai

CONTENTS

JAZZ IS LIVING MUSIC

Do you sing along with pop music? Play air guitar to a rock song? You may even twirl to the melodies of classical music. But do you know about the instruments, voices, and history that give jazz music its unique sound?

Jazz music has evolved over the years. The earliest jazz hit Americans' ears around the start of the 20th century, with small bands experimenting with new rhythms.

Billy Taylor
(1921–2010)

"Jazz is America's classical music."
—Billy Taylor
jazz composer, pianist, and teacher

These bands grew bigger, with people playing lively trumpets, saxophones, pianos, and drums. Today's jazz riffs may come from electronic instruments like electric guitars and synthesizers.

Change is in the nature of jazz. One song may never sound the same way twice. Each jazz musician develops their own style of playing that listeners can get to know.

Jazz music has inspired dance crazes, art, fashions, poetry, and more. So, what is jazz?

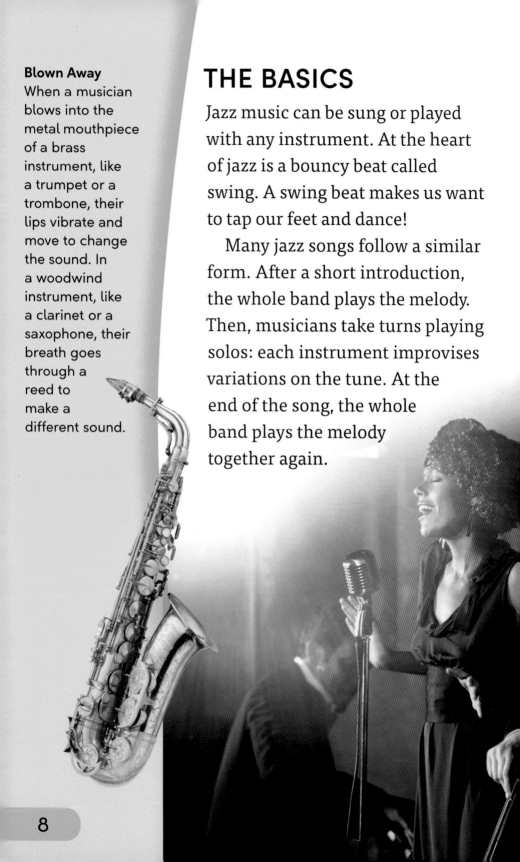

Blown Away
When a musician blows into the metal mouthpiece of a brass instrument, like a trumpet or a trombone, their lips vibrate and move to change the sound. In a woodwind instrument, like a clarinet or a saxophone, their breath goes through a reed to make a different sound.

THE BASICS

Jazz music can be sung or played with any instrument. At the heart of jazz is a bouncy beat called swing. A swing beat makes us want to tap our feet and dance!

Many jazz songs follow a similar form. After a short introduction, the whole band plays the melody. Then, musicians take turns playing solos: each instrument improvises variations on the tune. At the end of the song, the whole band plays the melody together again.

Another common element in jazz music is a call-and-response pattern. One musician sings or plays a melody, and another musician plays back an "answer." It's like a musical conversation between bandmates.

Ba-Dum! Rhythm instruments make sound when they are hit, pressed, or plucked. These instruments include the piano, bass, vibraphone, and drums. Their beats drive a song's speed, or tempo, while helping the band play together.

The main melody of a jazz song is recognizable each time it is played. However, many jazz songs include parts that are improvised, or made up as they are played.

DECADES OF JAZZ

1800s: Pre-jazz musical styles merge in Congo Square, New Orleans

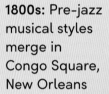

1900: Ragtime brings syncopated rhythms

Late 1800s: Early blues expresses emotions

1910s: Syncopated dance music heats up

Listen Up!
Check out these tunes to see how the jazz sound has changed over the decades.

"Memphis Blues"
James Reese Europe (1919)

"Struttin' with Some Barbecue"
Louis Armstrong (1927)

"Battle of Swing"
Duke Ellington (1938)

One type of improvised singing is called scatting. Instead of words, scatting uses fun, made-up words like "shoo-bee-doo-bee."

Musicians also improvise when they create a new version of a popular song. Songs that have been played and recorded by many artists are called standards.

1960s and beyond: Experimental styles change with the times

1920s: Jazz explodes in New Orleans and beyond

1940s: Swing gives way to bebop

1930s: Big bands rule the scene

1950s: Cool jazz relaxes and hard bop heats up

"A Night in Tunisia"
Charlie Parker (1946)

"So What"
Miles Davis (1959)

"Maiden Voyage"
Herbie Hancock (1965)

"Spain"
Chick Corea (1972)

"Black Codes"
Wynton Marsalis (1985)

"Respected Destroyer"
Terri Lyne Carrington (2022)

Park It!
The New Orleans Jazz National Historical Park celebrates jazz. You can join a drum circle or hear the park's rangers play jazz.

JAZZY BEGINNINGS

Though it's hard to say exactly when jazz music started, it's not hard to say where. Jazz became popular in the early 1900s in the diverse city of New Orleans, Louisiana. Several cultures influenced its sounds, but jazz music was created by Black Americans.

When slavery was practiced in America, slave owners feared that enslaved people might send each other messages about escaping.

Bamboula dancing, New Orleans, 1800s

Enslaved people were often not allowed to drum or speak their native languages.

But in Louisiana, the rules were different. In 1817, Congo Square in New Orleans became the gathering place for free and enslaved Black people. On Sundays, hundreds of people came there to buy and sell goods. They sang, clapped, and danced to bamboula drums and banjos. This musical mash-up created the rhythms at the heart of jazz.

Indigenous Influence
Early jazz music was also influenced by the Indigenous Houma people who lived near Congo Square. Today, Indigenous people still share their music at jazz festivals in New Orleans.

Listening Live
In the early 20th century, people could listen to recorded music on gramophones or self-playing pianos. Some bought copies of sheet music to play themselves. But most of the time, people watched live performances.

A trio of early American musical styles also influenced the sound of jazz.

Blues music was created by Southern Black Americans after the Civil War. Black spirituals and field calls of enslaved people influenced the blues. Blues songs are about the ups and downs of life. Blues can sound happy or sad. Jazz musicians borrowed this emotional style.

Gertrude "Ma" Rainey (1886–1939)
Ma Rainey was often called "the Mother of the Blues."

Bessie Smith (ca. 1894–1937)
Smith was known as "the Empress of the Blues."

Scott Joplin (1868–1917)
Joplin was considered "the King of Ragtime."

W. C. Handy (1873–1958)
Handy was known as "the Father of the Blues."

In the late 1800s, the ragtime style of piano music introduced an unexpected rhythmic pattern called syncopation. In ragtime, piano players use the left hand to keep a steady beat while the right hand plays a quick melody. This peppy rhythm caught the ear of early jazz musicians.

During the 1910s, small bands of musicians played popular songs at parades, picnics, and funerals. These bands featured cornets, clarinets, banjos, trombones, and drums. Early jazz was influenced by marching bands, too.

On the Record
In the late 1800s, the invention of the phonograph meant that music could be recorded and played back at another time. Loud brass and percussion instruments made better recordings than softer string instruments, so jazz was a popular style to record. The Original Dixieland Jazz Band made the first jazz record in 1917.

Joseph "King" Oliver (1885–1938)
King Oliver made his cornet "talk" with a "wah-wah" sound by using a mute, a device that muffles the tone. Like many Black musicians from New Orleans, he headed north to find work. Oliver's Creole Jazz Band took jazz to Chicago, Illinois. In 1922, Oliver landed a gig at Chicago's Lincoln Gardens, one of the first places outside the South to feature jazz.

Lil Hardin Armstrong (1898–1971)

Let's Go, Lil
In the 1920s, Armstrong's wife, Lil Hardin Armstrong managed his career. But Lil was more than Mrs. Armstrong! Before she met Louis, she was a singer in King Oliver's band. She played piano for Louis's Hot Five and later in her career became a musical director, a fashion designer, and a writer.

Louis Armstrong (1901–1971)
Louis Armstrong was born into poverty in New Orleans. He learned to play the cornet as a child. In 1922, King Oliver asked Armstrong to join his band in Chicago. Armstrong's improvised trumpet solos made him a star. His soulful melodies and rhythmic invention set a new standard for jazz. He used his unique, rumbly voice as an instrument, too, and was the first to record a scat solo, in "Heebie Jeebies."

In New Orleans, the neighborhood called Storyville was known for its music and nightlife. Pop-up bands in this part of town used things like cans and boxes to make their instruments. Musicians called out and joked with the audience.

Sidney Bechet (1897–1959)
Sidney Bechet started playing the clarinet when he was six years old. By the time he was in his teens, he was playing with some of the top bands in New Orleans. In 1919, Bechet joined the Southern Syncopated Orchestra on their European tour. In London, he bought a soprano saxophone, and for decades afterward, Bechet dazzled crowds with his saxophone's swinging sounds.

Listen Up!
Hear how ragtime, blues, and Dixieland jazz were the building blocks of a new American sound.

"Maple Leaf Rag"
Scott Joplin (1899)
"Tiger Rag"
The Original Dixieland Jazz Band (1917)
"Carolina Shout"
James P. Johnson (1921)

Many jazz musicians started out in Storyville. Louis Armstrong and Sidney Bechet were some of the first musicians to experiment with the loose, swinging sound that set jazz apart from ragtime.

Ferdinand "Jelly Roll" Morton (1890–1941)

"Dippermouth Blues"
King Oliver's Creole Jazz Band (1923)

"Wild Cat Blues"
Clarence Williams and Sidney Bechet (1923)

"St. Louis Blues"
Bessie Smith with Louis Armstrong (1925)

"Black Bottom Stomp"
Jelly Roll Morton (1926)

"West End Blues"
Louis Armstrong (1928)

The Great Migration
From the 1910s to the 1970s, millions of Black Americans moved from southern states to cities like Chicago, Detroit, New York, and Los Angeles, looking for new opportunities. Many jazz musicians migrated, too, chasing their dreams to the cities where jazz was thriving.

THE JAZZ AGE

The 1920s brought big changes in America. Women gained the right to vote, and cars and railroads made it easier to move between cities. Thanks to the new medium of radio, jazz music was the soundtrack to an era of prosperity and modernization.

Jazz got big in cities like Chicago and New York. Harlem, a primarily Black neighborhood in New York City, was a hot spot for Black culture, music, and arts.

Some of the most famous jazz bands came from the nightclubs in Harlem.

As jazz grew in popularity, the bands that played jazz grew, too. A typical big band, or jazz orchestra, had between 10 and 17 members. Soon, dance floors were ruled by big bands. And the bandleaders who conducted those bands became big stars.

On the Radio
Not every music lover could make it to big cities to hear the hottest jazz. Some people could listen to records at home. But when radios became more affordable, the jazz craze spread across the nation—and the world.

Mary Lou Williams (1910–1981)
Mary Lou Williams first joined a band at age 15, at a time when almost all jazz musicians were men. Her skill as a pianist, composer, and arranger earned her a spot with Andy Kirk and His Twelve Clouds of Joy, a top band in Kansas City. Williams helped shape the sound of the big band era. She wrote music for many bands. Later, she also taught young people about jazz to ensure that its roots in the Black community were not forgotten.

Black, Brown and Beige

In 1943, Duke Ellington conducted the first performance of his composition "Black, Brown and Beige." The music was about the struggles and triumphs of Black people in America. Ellington played the 45-minute piece for a diverse crowd from different races and backgrounds at Carnegie Hall in New York.

Duke Ellington (1899–1974)

Throughout his 50-year career, pianist, composer, and bandleader Duke Ellington was one of jazz's most influential leaders. The music he wrote for his orchestra was creative and colorful. It expressed a wide range of feeling and emotion. Radio broadcasts of his band's shows at the Cotton Club made Ellington a household name across the country. He composed more than 1,000 pieces. As trumpeter Wynton Marsalis once said of Ellington, "His music sounds like America."

Open to All
The Savoy Ballroom in Harlem welcomed both Black and white customers during a time when segregation was common. Night clubs like the Cotton Club featured Black artists onstage, but they served only white customers.

"Jazz is a heartbeat."
—Langston Hughes
writer and Harlem Renaissance leader

As jazz bands added speed and swing to their tunes, young people created new dances like the Charleston and the Lindy Hop.

Cab Calloway (1907–1994)
Bandleader Cab Calloway lit up the stage with his dancing and call-and-response singing. Calloway learned to scat from Louis Armstrong. He got audiences singing "Hi de hi de ho!" along with his most famous song, "Minnie the Moocher."

Benny Goodman and Count Basie, 1943

Benny Goodman (1909–1986)
By 1938, clarinetist Benny Goodman, known as "the King of Swing," was leading the most popular dance band in the nation. When he took his orchestra to play in a big theater where the audience could only sit and watch, no one was sure whether people would like it. But the concert at Carnegie Hall was a huge success. It helped prove that jazz was an art form and not just dance music.

Integration Takes the Stage
Goodman's 1938 concert was not just historic for musical reasons. Goodman, who was white, included Black musicians Teddy Wilson and Lionel Hampton during quartet pieces. Other Black players, like Count Basie and Lester Young, joined in for other songs. These were among the first racially integrated groups to perform in front of a paying audience.

Ella Fitzgerald (1917–1996)

When Ella Fitzgerald was 17, she sang during Amateur Night at Harlem's famous Apollo Theater, and the audience demanded an encore. Bandleader Chick Webb saw her onstage a year later and invited her to sing with his band. Her first record, "A–Tisket, A–Tasket," sold one million copies. Her vibrant voice and charisma earned her the nickname "the First Lady of Song."

Listen Up!

Can you pick out some of the instruments playing in these swing-era classics?

"Minnie the Moocher"
Cab Calloway (1931)

"It Don't Mean a Thing (If It Ain't Got That Swing)"
Duke Ellington (1932)

"Walkin and Swingin"
Andy Kirk and His Twelve Clouds of Joy, Mary Lou Williams (1936)

William James "Count" Basie (1904–1984)
Pianist and bandleader Count Basie led one of the
most swinging big bands of all time. The Count
Basie Orchestra moved from Kansas City, Missouri,
to New York City in the mid-1930s. They played
the blues with a relaxed and flowing beat. Their
arrangements were based on riffs—short, repeated
melodic and rhythmic ideas. Even after Basie died,
his band continued.

"One O' Clock Jump"
Count Basie (1937)

"Sing, Sing, Sing"
Benny Goodman and
His Orchestra (1938)

"A-Tisket, A-Tasket"
Ella Fitzgerald
with Chick Webb (1938)

"Take the 'A' Train"
Duke Ellington (1941)

Helen Jones Woods (1923–2020)

Teen Titan
Helen Jones Woods was a teen trombone player with the International Sweethearts of Rhythm. This group of teen girls was the first interracial women's band in the US. Even while touring in segregated places, the young band drew large crowds of both Black and white fans.

OFF TO WAR

From 1939 to 1945, World War II turned the world—and the American jazz scene—upside down. Gas shortages and curfews stopped music tours. Factories switched from making instruments and jukeboxes to military goods.

The International Sweethearts of Rhythm

After the US entered the war in 1941, men had to register for the military draft, so they could be called to serve in the war at any time. Musicians like Dave Brubeck and John Coltrane were drafted into the armed services.

As men went off to war, jazz bands in the US became smaller. And female performers stepped into the spotlight.

Alberta Hunter
(1895–1984)

Travel Musicians
Music lifted the soldiers' spirits. The United Service Organizations (USO) brought thousands of musicians and entertainers to play for soldiers overseas. Among them, jazz singer Alberta Hunter led a group of performers called the Rhythm Rascals, putting on shows for troops in India.

Swing music played its own part in the conflict. American troops stationed abroad were cheered by the sounds they had loved at home. Some jazz greats were part of the war effort themselves.

Glenn Miller (1904–1944)
When popular big band leader Glenn Miller joined the army in 1942, he put together a large Army Air Force Band. The band played hundreds of shows for troops in the US and Europe. In December of 1944, Miller boarded a military plane that disappeared over the English Channel, and he was never seen again. But the Glenn Miller Orchestra still exists today.

Listen Up!
Hear the swinging sounds that helped boost spirits during wartime and beyond.

"In the Mood"
Glenn Miller Orchestra (1939)

"My Castle's Rockin'"
Alberta Hunter (1940)

"Boogie Woogie Bugle Boy"
The Andrews Sisters (1941)

Josephine Baker (1906–1975)

American jazz singer and dancer Josephine Baker joined the French military to act as a spy. Baker was famous in France, and she used her celebrity status to get important people to tell her their secrets. She smuggled documents and carried sheet music with secret messages written in invisible ink.

"A Slip of the Lip"
Duke Ellington (1942)

"(I've Got a Gal in) Kalamazoo"
Glenn Miller (1942)

"Brazil"
Josephine Baker (1944)

"Swing Shift"
International Sweethearts
of Rhythm (1944)

"G.I. Jive"
Johnny Mercer (1944)

Edmond Hall, Emmett Berry, and Snub Mosley playing on CBS Radio, 1942

SINGING IS IN

In the 1940s, a wartime tax made it very expensive for American clubs to allow dancing. This was bad news for big swing bands, but good news for small groups and singers.

Also at this time, the musicians' union went on strike. Musicians refused to make records until they got paid royalties, or money for each time their records were sold. But singers could still make records, and instrumentalists were allowed to perform live on the radio.

Billie Holiday (1915–1959)
Singer Billie Holiday rose to fame during the 1930s in the nightclubs of Harlem. Her voice had an emotional, melancholy quality. She improvised melodies like a horn player. She became best known for "Strange Fruit," a heartbreaking song about violent attacks on Black Americans in the South.

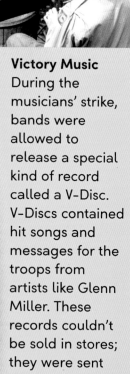

Between the tax and the strike, big bands began to fade away as solo singers stepped into the spotlight.

Sarah Vaughan (1924–1990)

After winning an amateur contest at the Apollo Theater, Sarah Vaughan was hired as a big band singer, and then she began a solo career. Vaughan's incredible vocal range— her ability to sing from very low notes to very high ones—amazed her fans. She was also a master of scat singing. Known as "the Divine One," she dazzled audiences for almost 50 years.

Victory Music
During the musicians' strike, bands were allowed to release a special kind of record called a V-Disc. V-Discs contained hit songs and messages for the troops from artists like Glenn Miller. These records couldn't be sold in stores; they were sent overseas to encourage American soldiers in the war.

Some silky-voiced male singers known as crooners drew crowds to nightclubs and theaters. By the 1950s, almost half of Americans owned a television, and TV variety shows brought these smooth voices into people's living rooms.

Frank Sinatra (1915–1998)
Frank Sinatra was known for swinging versions of standard songs and romantic ballads. His expressive voice and sincerity singing love songs melted audiences' hearts.

Listen Up!
Enjoy the smooth sounds of these famous voices.

"All of Me"
Billie Holiday (1941)

"Straighten Up and Fly Right"
Nat King Cole (1943)

"Lullaby of Birdland"
Sarah Vaughan (1954)

Samara Joy
(1999–)

Modern Crooners
Singers like Leslie Odom Jr., Harry Connick Jr., Michael Bublé, Diana Krall, Cécile McLorin Salvant, and Samara Joy keep the vocal sounds coming.

Nat King Cole (1919–1965)
Before he was 20, jazz singer and pianist Nat King Cole had formed a musical trio. His warm voice charmed Black and white audiences alike. His classic 1946 recording of "The Christmas Song" remains a popular holiday standard. In 1956, Cole was the first Black American to host a nationally broadcast TV show.

"In the Wee Small Hours of the Morning"
Frank Sinatra (1955)

"The Way You Look Tonight"
Michael Bublé (2003)

"Autumn Leaves"
Leslie Odom Jr. (2014)

"I've Got Your Number"
Cécile McLorin Salvant (2017)

"Love Is Here to Stay"
Tony Bennett and Diana Krall (2018)

"Stardust"
Samara Joy (2020)

THE PIZAZZ OF AFRO-CUBAN JAZZ

In the 1940s, people from Cuba were moving to New York for better job opportunities, and they brought their music along. Afro-Cuban jazz blended Cuban, African, and big band jazz rhythms.

Afro-Cuban orchestras played with popular American jazz instruments and Latin rhythm instruments, like the congas and maracas. Performers sang in English or Spanish. These bands played in dance halls, like the Park Palace Ballroom in Spanish Harlem.

By the 1960s, Puerto Rican and Latin American musicians brought their influence to Afro-Cuban jazz. Today, this music is called Latin jazz.

José Mangual Sr. and Mario Bauzá

Chano Pozo
(1915–1948)

Fancy Footwork
Chano Pozo co-wrote and performed "Manteca" with Dizzy Gillespie. Pozo drummed and danced at the same time, using moves he learned at Cuban festivals.

Graciela Pérez
Gutiérrez
(1915–2010)

Frank "Machito" Grillo (ca. 1908–1984)

Singer Machito Grillo, known simply as Machito, moved from Cuba to Harlem in 1937. Machito teamed up with Cuban musician Mario Bauzá to start the band Machito and His Afro-Cubans. They recorded the first Afro-Cuban jazz record. Machito's foster sister Graciela (who also went by just one name) joined the band as a scat singer. Graciela became known as "the First Lady of Latin Jazz."

Listen Up!
Listen for the clave and other percussion instruments in these hits.

"Tanga"
Machito and
His Afro-Cubans (1942)

"Manteca"
Dizzy Gillespie featuring
Chano Pozo (1947)

Tito Puente (1923–2000)

Tito Puente was born in Spanish Harlem to Puerto Rican parents. By age 13, he was a professional musician. Later, he would be known as "the King of Latin Jazz." Puente played timbale drums with Machito's band before starting his own band. Over a 50-year career, Puente recorded 118 records and won 6 Grammys. Today, Spanish Harlem has a street named after him.

The Heartbeat

The clave is a rhythm woven through much of Latin jazz. It's made by tapping together a pair of wooden sticks called claves to create a two- and three-beat pattern, like a beating heart inside the songs.

"Oyéme Mamá"
Machito featuring
Graciela (1954)

"Afro Blue"
Mongo Santamaria (1959)

"Oye Como Va"
Tito Puente (1962)

"Silencio"
Miguel Zenon (2011)

"Vámonos Pa'l Monte"
Eddie Palmieri (2018)

TO BEBOP OR NOT TO BEBOP

By the mid-1940s, some musicians felt restricted by big bands. Smaller groups gave them more freedom to improvise. They developed a creative new style called "bebop." It featured more complex harmonies and rhythms. It was often played at fast tempos. Bebop players thought of themselves as artists, not entertainers.

Thinking Up Words
In vocalese, people wrote lyrics to match the instrumental solos of popular jazz tunes. Groups like Lambert, Hendricks, and Ross (above) delivered tongue-twisting lyrics at astonishing speed.

Charlie "Bird" Parker (1920–1955)
Saxophonist Charlie Parker left his hometown of Kansas City for New York, where he became one of the the most influential soloists in jazz history. With Dizzy Gillespie and a few others, Parker invented the musical language of bebop. The unpredictable twists and turns of his solos still startle and influence musicians today.

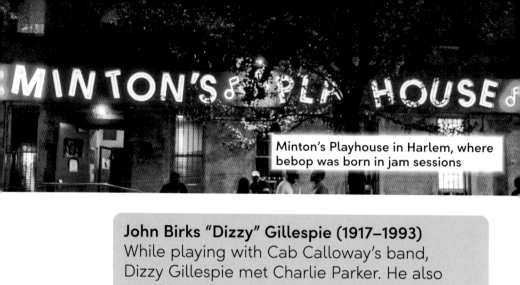

Minton's Playhouse in Harlem, where bebop was born in jam sessions

John Birks "Dizzy" Gillespie (1917–1993)
While playing with Cab Calloway's band, Dizzy Gillespie met Charlie Parker. He also met Mario Bauzá and became interested in Afro-Cuban jazz. Gillespie led both small groups and big bands. When he played the trumpet, his cheeks rounded like balloons. He was known for using a trumpet that was bent at a sharp angle, but it was his playing technique and charisma that made him a star.

Influential Teacher

Dizzy Gillespie, Charlie Parker, Thelonious Monk, Art Blakey, Miles Davis, and many more jazz stars had something in common (besides a love of jazz!). They were all taught and mentored by Mary Lou Williams.

Thelonious Monk (1917–1982)

Pianist and composer Thelonious Monk influenced bebop, but his music was different. It was full of odd rhythms, unusual melodies, and surprising silence. His songs could be playful. They could also be hard for audiences to understand at first. Many of his songs, like "Round Midnight" and "Blue Monk," became jazz standards.

In the mid-1950s, bebop gave way to hard bop. Hard bop was fast but not as wild as bebop. It drew from the soulful sounds of rhythm and blues and gospel music, and it returned to a classic, more danceable swing rhythm. The shorter songs still left room for improvised solos.

Listen Up!
Try to keep up with these quick bebop and hard bop tunes!

"Dizzy Atmosphere"
Dizzy Gillespie and Charlier Parker (1945)

"A Night in Tunisia"
Charlie Parker (1946)

"Now's the Time"
Charlie Parker (1953)

Art Blakey (1919–1990)

As a seventh grader, Art Blakey was already playing piano with dance bands. Later, he switched to drums. Blakey was all about rhythm. He drove his band with a big, swinging beat. He led the Jazz Messengers from the mid-1950s until his death in 1990. Blakey was famous for hiring the best young talent, including Freddie Hubbard, Wayne Shorter, and brothers Wynton and Branford Marsalis.

Sonny Rollins (1930–)

Sonny Rollins grew up in Harlem. He started playing saxophone in his teens and performed into his 80s. Rollins is known for the creativity of his improvisations and playing multiple improvisations and for making old songs sound fresh. From 1959 through 1961, Rollins stopped performing onstage but practiced for many hours every day on the Williamsburg Bridge.

"Blue Monk"
Thelonious Monk (1954)

"St. Thomas"
Sonny Rollins (1956)

"Moanin'"
Art Blakey and the
Jazz Messengers (1958)

"Cloudburst"
Lambert, Hendricks,
and Ross (1959)

"Nica's Dream"
Horace Silver (1960)

Kind of Blue
Miles Davis's 1959 album *Kind of Blue* is the best-selling jazz album of all time.

COOL GETS HOT

The intensity of bebop wasn't for everyone. Some musicians started experimenting with slower tempos and a more mellow feel, and cool jazz was born. Cool jazz used a wider range of instruments and more formal arrangements. Cool jazz was a natural fit for the laid-back lifestyle in California, so it's also known as West Coast jazz.

1958 *Esquire* magazine photo featuring 57 of Harlem's greatest jazz musicians

44

Recording session for *Birth of the Cool*, January 21, 1949

Miles Davis (1926–1991)

Miles Davis moved to New York from St. Louis to study at the Juilliard School. But he dropped out to play bebop and join Charlie Parker's band. In 1949, Davis put together a group to play arrangements by Gil Evans and others. These songs were recorded and later released as an album called *Birth of the Cool*. Davis defined hard bop in the '50s, pushed jazz forward in the '60s, and pioneered electric jazz-rock in the '70s and '80s.

The Modern Jazz Quartet

The Modern Jazz Quartet played a unique style of jazz that sometimes sounded like classical music but with a strong blues feeling. Pianist and composer John Lewis was the group's music director. Vibraphonist Milt Jackson was its most exciting soloist.

Chet Baker (1929–1988)

Trumpeter Chet Baker's soft vocals and romantic style of playing earned him the nickname "the Prince of Cool." Baker played in bands in high school and the army before joining the jazz scene. He worked with Charlie Parker in Los Angeles. With Gerry Mulligan's quartet, Baker recorded "My Funny Valentine," a song that became one of his top hits.

Gerry Mulligan (1927–1996)

Listen Up!
You may recognize some of these cool classics and famous jazz tunes.

"Boplicity"
Miles Davis (1949)

"Subconscious-Lee"
Lennie Tristano and Lee Konitz (1949)

"Over the Rainbow"
Shorty Rogers and His Giants (1951)

Dave Brubeck (1920–2012)

Dave Brubeck started playing piano at the age of four. He studied classical composition before shifting to jazz, and he liked to weave classical elements into his songs. He experimented with unusual rhythms and key changes. Brubeck was one of the most popular musicians in jazz for decades.

Cool Jazz Cartoons
A number of jazz artists composed music for TV and movie soundtracks. West Coast jazz pioneer Shorty Rogers played trumpet in the cartoon "The Three Little Bops." Pianist Vince Guaraldi composed music for *Peanuts* cartoons.

"My Funny Valentine"
Gerry Mulligan and Chet Baker (1952)

"Django"
Modern Jazz Quartet (1954)

"Take Five"
Dave Brubeck (1959)

"All Blues"
Miles Davis (1959)

"Round Midnight"
Art Pepper (1959)

"Linus and Lucy"
Vince Guaraldi Trio (1964)

THE SHAPE OF JAZZ

During the 1960s, many people began pushing back against rules and expectations for social behavior. At the same time, some musicians were finding freedom in new styles of jazz.

Beat Poetry
Jazz influenced a group of young writers called beat poets. The flowing improvisations of jazz inspired long and winding poems and prose. Writers like Jack Kerouac (above) sometimes sounded like they might be composing on the spot, just like jazz musicians.

Ornette Coleman (1930–2015)
Saxophonist Ornette Coleman believed in musical freedom. He played a raspy plastic saxophone on his album *The Shape of Jazz to Come*. This launched a new style called free jazz, in which musicians may ignore traditional rules of musical structure. But you can still hear the blues in Coleman's music.

Cecil Taylor (1929–2018)
Cecil Taylor was a classically trained pianist, yet as a jazz artist he played in a very untraditional style. He might touch the keys delicately with his fingertips or slam them with his palms, elbows, and forearms. He used the piano almost as if it were a set of drums, sometimes hitting it so hard that he broke keys or strings.

Herbie Hancock (1940–)

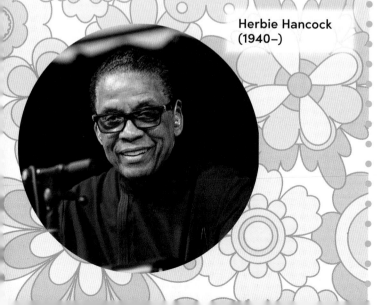

"Jazz is in the moment."
—**Herbie Hancock**
composer, piano player, actor, jazz ambassador, and teacher

Larry Coryell (1943–2017)

Jazz Powers Up

In the late 1960s and the 1970s, elements of rock, funk, and electronic dance music came together in a new sound called jazz fusion. Electronic instruments gave this style a modern feel. Larry Coryell was known as the "Godfather of Jazz Fusion."

Sun Ra (1914–1993)

Avant-garde music doesn't stick to traditional forms and rules. Sun Ra was an avant-garde jazz musician who was inspired by the ancient past and the future. He composed challenging pieces for unusual instruments. Elements like ancient Egyptian dances, chants, and even martial arts came together in his out-of-this-world performances.

John Coltrane (1926–1967)

Saxophonist, bandleader, and composer John Coltrane learned from stars like Miles Davis and Thelonious Monk. He played bebop and hard bop before experimenting with new ideas and, eventually, free jazz. Coltrane became famous for long, expressive solos, some lasting up to 30 minutes. He also made music with his wife, Alice, who played the piano and harp.

Alabama

In 1963, a church in Birmingham, Alabama, was bombed. Four young Black girls died in the bombing. Two months later, John Coltrane recorded a song called "Alabama." This grief-filled song has been inspiring people in the fight for equal rights for 60 years.

John Coltrane and Dizzy Gillespie, 1951

Alice McLeod Coltrane (1937–2007)

Around this time, more people began to demand equal freedoms for Black Americans. A lot of jazz musicians used their performances to speak out for change.

Max Roach (1924–2007)
In 1960, drummer Max Roach, his wife, singer Abbey Lincoln, and others recorded "We Insist! Freedom Now Suite." In the midst of the civil rights movement in America, this album addressed injustices against Black people in both the US and Africa.

The Fight to Be Seen
Saxophone player Rahsaan Roland Kirk founded the Jazz and People's Movement. This group led protests to get more Black jazz musicians on TV and to ensure that they were fairly paid.

Abbey Lincoln (1930–2010)

Rahsaan Roland Kirk (1935–1977)

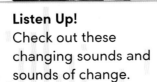

Listen Up!
Check out these changing sounds and sounds of change.

"Sun Song"
Sun Ra (1957)

"Fables of Faubus"
Charles Mingus (1959)

"Freedom Day"
Max Roach (1960)

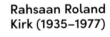

Charles Mingus (1922–1979)

In 1954, the Supreme Court ruled that segregation in schools was unconstitutional. But the governor of Arkansas used the military to keep Black students from attending a white school. Bassist Charles Mingus wrote a song called "Fables of Faubus" to protest the racism and violence of this action.

Freedom Rides

In 1961, Black and white people rode buses through the southern states to protest segregation laws. Riders were often attacked by angry mobs or arrested. Art Blakey inspired these protesters with a song called "The Freedom Rider."

Nina Simone (1933–2003)

Nina Simone used her voice to shake up the world. Even as a child, she refused to play her first recital until her parents, who had been moved to the back of the hall, were allowed to sit in the front row. In the 1968 song "Revolution," she encouraged Black Americans to take a stand against injustice.

"My Favorite Things"
John Coltrane (1961)

"Adam's Apple"
Wayne Shorter (1966)

"Tales (8 Whisps)"
Cecil Taylor (1966)

"Four Women"
Nina Simone (1966)

"Tell Me a Bedtime Story"
Herbie Hancock (1969)

"Ain't No Sunshine"
Rahsaan Roland Kirk (1972)

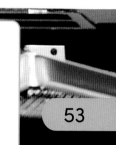

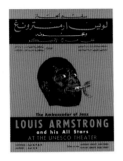

WHERE IN THE WORLD IS JAZZ?

Musicians across the globe added their own cultural twists to this American form of music.

Jazz Ambassadors

In 1956, the American government started sending jazz musicians on world tours. The US hoped to introduce international audiences to American culture. They also wanted to gain other countries' support during the Cold War era.

Django Reinhardt (1910–1953)

Guitarist Django Reinhardt formed the first all-string jazz band in Paris, France, in the 1930s. The band blended French, Romani, and American music to create the unique harmonies of jazz manouche. Reinhardt, whose left hand had been badly burned in a fire, plucked speedy solos using only two fingers!

Reinhardt with Duke Ellington, 1946

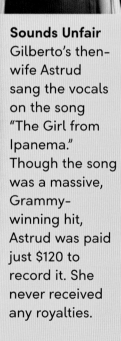

Sounds Unfair
Gilberto's then-wife Astrud sang the vocals on the song "The Girl from Ipanema." Though the song was a massive, Grammy-winning hit, Astrud was paid just $120 to record it. She never received any royalties.

João Gilberto (1931–2019)
Brazilian guitarist and singer João Gilberto was a pioneer in bossa nova, a new sound inspired by cool jazz and samba rhythms. In 1964, Gilberto recorded an album with American guitarist Stan Getz. *Getz/Gilberto* won the Grammy for Album of the Year.

Today, jazz is performed and celebrated all over the world! Many cities host jazz festivals each year. Listeners of all ages dance and sing with other fans.

Damez Nababan at
Java Jazz Festival, 2019

Listen Up!
Do these international sounds of jazz make you want to dance?

"Nuages"
Django Reinhardt (1940)
"Bim Bom"
João Gilberto (1958)

Countries that created new jazz styles—like Brazil, Cuba, and France—have large jazz festivals in their capital cities. Jazz festivals are held in many other cities, too—from Tokyo, Japan, to Cape Town, South Africa.

World Record
One of the biggest jazz events in the world is the annual Montreal International Jazz Festival in Montreal, Canada. In 2004, a world record-breaking two million people attended!

Yuri Mahatma performing at the Java Jazz Festival, Jakarta, Indonesia, 2019

"The Girl from Ipanema"
Stan Getz, João Gilberto, Astrud Gilberto (1963)

"Mannenberg"
Abdullah Ibrahim (1974)

"Long Yellow Road"
Toshiko Akiyoshi (1974)

JAZZ LIVES TODAY

Jazz is always changing. Today, jazz musicians are experimenting more than ever.

Esperanza Spalding (1984–)

As a little girl, after Esperanza Spalding saw Yo Yo Ma playing cello on *Mister Rogers' Neighborhood*, she decided to learn the violin. She tried out many different instruments before settling on the upright bass. In 2011, Spalding became the first jazz musician to win the Grammy for Best New Artist. She sings and plays bass as she leads her own band, and she has collaborated with living legends of jazz as well as with pop and R & B stars.

Makaya McCraven (1983–)
Makaya McCraven was born in Paris in 1983 to musician parents. He is known for his lively drum solos. McCraven calls himself a "beat scientist," mixing jazz with the beats of hip-hop and funk. On McCraven's 2021 album, he put a modern spin on classic songs by Art Blakey, Horace Silver, and others.

An exhibit of album covers at the American Jazz Museum, Kansas City, Missouri

Jammin' in April
In 2001, the Smithsonian National Museum of American History kicked off National Jazz Appreciation Month (aptly shortened to JAM) with an 18-member jam session.

Jazz is for everyone. You can enjoy it in all the places you go.

At home, you can attend a virtual jazz festival. Every year, cities like New Orleans and Montreal host jazz events that are streamed online.

Your teacher could set up a virtual field trip to the American Jazz Museum in Kansas City.

Listen Up!
Can you hear influences of early jazz in these newer tunes?

"Boogety Boogety"
Kenny Garrett (2011)

"Sheik of Araby /
I Found a New Baby (medley)"
Jason Moran (2014)

"Unconditional Love"
Esperanza Spalding (2016)

You can watch a jazzy movie or have a dance contest in your living room. There's no right or wrong way to enjoy jazz. Just improvise!

Jazz for You

You may have heard jazz music in movies! The hip solos in *The Princess and the Frog* recall the Jazz Age in New Orleans. *Soul*'s main character is a jazz pianist. In *Sing!* the rat croons a Frank Sinatra standard. Enjoy Brazilian jazz in Rio or the Vince Guaraldi Trio's tunes in *A Charlie Brown Christmas.*

"Put On a Happy Face"
JD Allen (2018)

"Bigger Than Us"
Jon Batiste (2020)

"Evoorg"
Tom Harrell (2020)

"Sunset"
Makaya McCraven (2021)

"Mae West: Advice"
Darcy James Argue's Secret Society with Cécile McLorin Salvant (2023)

GLOSSARY

Amateur
A person who does something without training; a beginner

Ambassador
A person who represents a country while visiting other places

Arrangement
Music that is written or adapted to be played or sung by a variety of instruments or voices

Bamboula
A West African drum; a dance performed to the beat of this drum

Civil rights
Rights that promise equal opportunities and fair treatment for all people regardless of their race, sex, gender, religion, or nationality

Cold War
From the 1945 to 1991, a time of political tension between the US and the Soviet Union

Compose
To create and write down a piece of music

Harmony
Different musical notes that sound good together; a tune that complements the melody

Improvisation
Making up music while performing it

Melody
A song's main tune

Pioneer
One of the first people to do something

Professional
Someone who gets paid to do a job or activity

Rhythm
A pattern of beats

Royalties
Payments made to musicians when their music is sold, streamed, or used on radio, television, or in movies

Scatting
Improvised singing with made-up words and sounds

Solo
Part of a song that's played or sung by one musician

Standard
A widely popular song played or recorded by different musicians

Strike
Stopping a job or activity to demand changes in working conditions

Syncopation
Making an off beat stand out in a steady, repeated rhythm

Tempo
The speed of a piece of music

INDEX

QUIZ

Answer the questions to see what you have learned. Check your answers in the key below.

1. True or false: Jazz music always sounds the same.

2. What is the city in Louisiana known as the birthplace of jazz?

3. What do we call jazz singing with made-up words?

4. Which two musicians are considered the creators of bebop?

5. Which style of Brazilian jazz was inspired by cool jazz and samba rhythms?

1. False 2. New Orleans 3. Scatting
4. Charlie Parker and Dizzy Gillespie 5. Bossa nova